Broken Rhythms

Elizabeth Selden

BROKEN RHYTHMS

ISBN: 9798862712513

Independently Published

A NOTE TO THE READER

These poems have been gathered over many years, many different traumas, explorations in healing and life experiences. I share them with you, these darkest and brightest moments, with the hope that your soul's ache may somehow feel a connection with another's. With my desire to reach your shadow self, to shine an embracing light around it, and provide a beacon…a way out of the darkness. And to sing to you that you are not alone!

You have permission to weep,
to rage, to tear at the fabric of reality.
You have permission to scream,
to whisper, to wonder and to wish.
You have permission to question,
to start over, to change the world.
You do not have permission to give up.
You are too valuable. Too precious.
You are the only you there
has ever been or will ever be.
Only you can change the world
in the way you will.
Feel. Breathe. Live.
I see you.
I love you.

CONTENTS

BROKEN RHYTHMS

BROKEN RHYTHMS

1 THE BEGINNING

In the beginning there was the void.
Emptiness.
Stillness.
Silence.

And in less than the time it takes to
Sigh.
Life.
Death.
Eternity.

Cycling
Cycling
Cycling

Until a new void swallows the old.

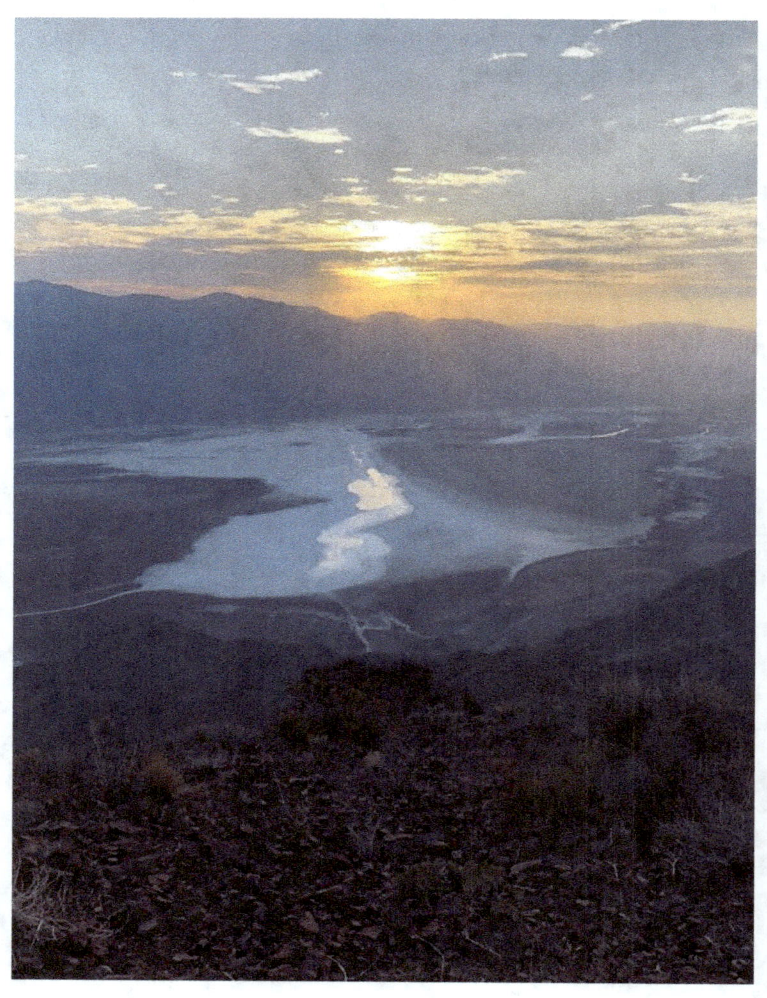

Death Valley 2018

ONCE UPON A TIME

Once upon a time.
It is here that stories begin.
Life, death and everything
in between comes after
these long-spoken words.

Tales of great warriors
are spun within the pages
of tales shared by ancestors
around a glowing fire as
smoking embers glow red.

Stories of adversity and
triumph echo through time's
ancient ears, buried in the soil
and hanging in the mists
surrounding great bards.

Poems of the lost and
shattered souls we have
almost forgotten sometimes
rise up from the shadows, eerie
and dark, tales of sorrow.

Through the whispered words
of those who weep, sing
or rage, tales are born, webs
are woven and we hear as we
did once upon a time.

KEEPING TIME

She watched.
She paid no attention to
the world moving about her.

She counted
the red second hand's clicks
around and around on the big gray clock.

She did not notice
the seasons changing
or when one year turned to many.

Only the seconds.

Each one was as important
as the next.
She dared not miss a single one.

She never wasted a second,
storing year upon year with
purposed passion.

Watching the red second hand
going around and around
on the big gray clock.

One morning
the clock stopped.

She persevered.
Tick tick ticking as she kept time's
memories moving on.

THE OCEAN

I've never seen the ocean.
I sometimes have dreams about what it would be like.
Lots of white sand and and blue blue water.
And birds flying overhead.

I visit my ocean on rainy days especially.
I like the soft sounds and salty smell.
The sand is soft, cushioning my bare feet.
I can sink my toes into the cool, clear water.
A big fish and a little fish tickle my toes.

I've never seen the ocean.
I sometimes imagine the waves slap slapping against the rocks.
I hear the winds howling as birds scream and scream.
I choke on coarse sand.

On those days, the skies are dark
And the water is black and frightening.
The big fish swallows the little fish
And tears at my toes beneath the water.
I open my eyes and the
Darkness pulls me deep within.

I've never seen the ocean.
I sometimes wonder if it would appear as within my mind.
The sand, the rocks, the water and the fish.
And the birds flying overhead.

I sometimes wonder why I remember the darkness.
And I try to envision the water gently soaking into the sand
Or the waves rolling easily against one another.
But I always awaken to the storm.

THE SPIDER

Quickly crossing over my
windowpane, a tiny spider
catches my attention.

It pauses a single
moment...its delicate
legs exploring the sticker
I have placed there.

A motion of habit, I choose a shoe.

It senses danger as I
move into a position
of attack.

I ponder how many
intricate webs it has
created in its short life.

If it has made more of
an impact in the world
than I.

It makes a run for the corner's refuge.

My shoe comes down
sharply
and with a mind
operating instinctively.

I wait until there is no sign
of movement.
Tissue and a flush
eliminates an existence.

REFLECTION

The mirror does not
let me see
more than you see.

I lean closer to
the reflection.

We touch cold noses
and then the
me I see pulls away.

I watch a tear
trickle down
to her mouth.

My cheeks burn
fiery and wet.

I must not let it fall
to oblivion.

My tongue reaches
out too late.

When I look again
my reflection is
gone.

WITHOUT YOU

Loss rips at the fabric of
my reality, glistening in
the corner of my eyes
and following the curves
of my life's gnarled path.

Reflection requires every
muscle in my body,
aching, stretching to
almost breaking, and cruelly
reveals only my newest reality.

Without you.

I squint into the future.
Days and weeks and months
of clouded vision
fill my scattered thoughts,
enabling my apathy.

I do not move, barely
breathing for fear that
I might inhale more pain
than I can endure in this
hollow shell that remains.

Without you.

But what would you
say to me in this moment?
Your encouragement to
"live, love, laugh" would not
be enough. You've left me
to attempt it alone.

And so I continue to
mourn your missing
countenance, weeping
as nature's cruel cycle of
life leaves me here.

Without you.

STEEL

This shouldn't be happening.
It was the middle of the day
and she was surrounded by
a train car full of people.

He had entered at the last stop
and made eye contact with her.
He was tall. Wearing a black
trench coat and black boots.

Although she looked away,
he selected the empty row
behind her. The hair on the
back of her neck prickled.

"Don't move or I'll cut you."
His voice was rough and he
stank of cigarettes and whiskey.
Her stomach turned wildly.

She felt something cold and
sharp pricking at her side
as he leaned in closer, his
sour hair upon her cheek.

The train continued to race
along the tracks, the city
flashing by, travelers moving
from place to place, oblivious.

"I don't know you. Please
leave me alone," she said
the words she had been taught,
willing someone to help her.

BROKEN RHYTHMS

No one turned her direction.
Strangers fiercely studied windows
as his knife traced her side.
"I'm going to strip you naked."

"I'm going to paint you blue
and hang you from my ceiling.
After I'm done cutting you.
You're my art. You're dead."

Desperation pierced her.
The doors opened and he
seized her neck, pulling
her toward the platform.

Pleading for help again
she slipped out of his
grasp for just a moment as
the doors began to close.

Pulling the emergency switch,
he reached out again for her
throat, not even bothering
to conceal the glistening blade.

Alarms began to scream
and strangers looked away
turning pages, barely breathing,
silently recusing themselves.

The conductor approached and
he was gone, his terrible
fingerprints still upon her throat
and his stink still in her nose.

The doors closed after him and
she gagged, weeping to the
soothing sound of the train
clicking along the tracks.

DARKNESS

Gray. And there was snow.
Like a neglected television screen.
Only she couldn't turn it off.

She brought a heavy and trembling hand
to her swollen face. It was numb, her face.
She closed her eye to get rid of the snow.

Her throat was raw.
Like when a person coughs too much
and it hurts to swallow.

Only she hadn't been coughing.
She tasted blood, stale and metallic.
She tried not to gag and turned her head
the only direction it would move.

She opened her purple eye.
The snow came back, her ears, thundering.
She knew it had been hours.

Perhaps she should wait.
Wait for someone to notice she was there,
bleeding, swollen and broken.
She gingerly pulled herself to her feet.

The room spun, listlessly casting her
towards the doorway which she knew was
just beyond her reality.

He would not hurt her again.
She vowed, falling to her knees and
realizing the harshness of this truth as
she plunged once again into darkness.

2 THE JOURNEY

I have walked many miles
in tattered shoes.
Eyes cast down, ashamed of
what I had become.

A shadow, I was living a
life of faded reflections.
Lost in shattered mirrors
I had not broken.

Bound in my misery,
I could not see the light in
the darkness through
battered and swollen eyes.

I could not decipher the
earth from the sky,
clawing deeper into my
flooding and festering grave.

Until I was ready to climb out
…and live.

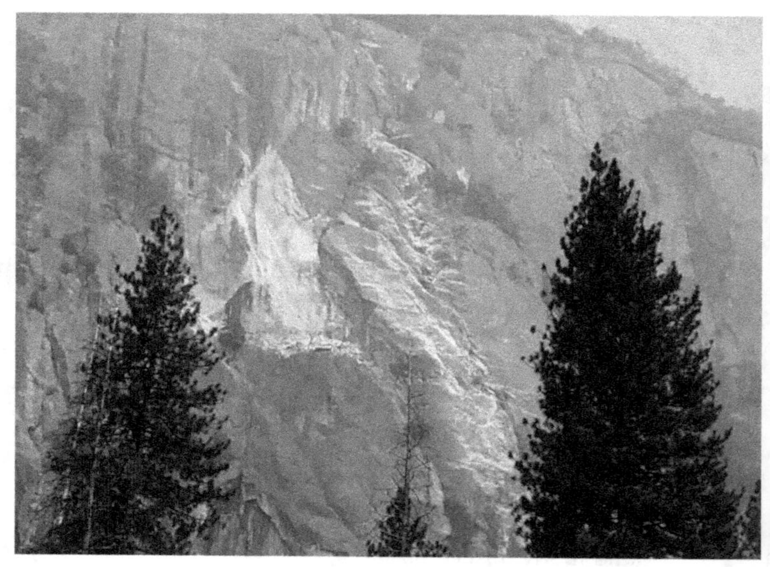

Yosemite 2018

CELEBRATING YOUR BIRTHDAY

Today is your birthday.
You would have been
One year older
One year wiser
One year more beautiful.

Today is your birthday.
The celebration
of your first day.
And the mourning
of your last.

Today
I cannot see your face
Or hear your voice
Or feel your touch.
And I weep for
my loss
and yours.

You missed the rising of
a year's worth of suns
and as many moons.
You missed the memories
made without you.

Today is your birthday.
And while some speak of peace
and heaven,
I sorrow earthbound,
Until we may hold one another
Again.

SILENCE

My humiliation feeds you
and my suffering,
hastens your potency.

I am bound to silence.
My burden. My weapon
against your ever

More frequent attacks
to my body and my mind.
Changing reality.

My prison is my own.
Built from violence, it
protects my soul.

The storm rages outside
my sanctuary.
For you cannot enter.

Within, I am safe.
The quiet songs of streams
are soft comfort.

Outside, the storm.
Within, silence offers
a peaceful embrace.

PREY

I am hunted.
A hapless beast driven
by instinct and fear.
Will I find refuge?

I call out.
The echoes of solitude
ripple in my ears.
In terror, I freeze.

My heart aches
with the realization that it
may have only a few more
seconds to beat.

Despair overtakes me.
The hunter has a keen eye
and unwavering aim.
I am in his sights.

Struck by his carefully planned
attack, I am wounded and
pleading as he takes aim
once again.

My cries pierce through the
endless night, falling
dull on brick and wooden,
bloody planks.

He finds my body's treasures
and greedily tears them
strand from strand
until I am silent.

ALONE

I close my eyes
as raining blows fall
again upon me.

The hours seem
a little shorter when
I cannot see you.

I pray that upon
opening them the
terror will be gone.

And I will awaken
alone.

THE STORM

Trapped within my racing mind
and uncooperative body
I cannot breathe.

Reflexes take over my being,
my consciousness, in this moment
of intense sensation.

I am at the heart of the storm
knowing the worst is
coming for me.

Knowing. Knowing. Knowing.
There is no way to breathe
or think or move.

The moment is collapsing
upon me, sucking me in.
Drowning. Suffocating.

Time stops. The past, present
and future cast their weight
upon me and

I am immobilized. Trapped. Lost.
Isolated in an airless glass cage,
I am in despair.

Loathing my helplessness, I am
its prisoner. Captive and complicit
I wait in terror.

The storm organizes its chaos.
The cyclone spins in wild patterns
I cannot battle.

BROKEN RHYTHMS

As the winds begin to tear at my
very essence, I brace myself
for will come next.

Raging against imminent death
it is the storm against my sanity.
Can I emerge unscathed?

Cast into the debris and dodging
shrapnel as it pierces my bleeding soul,
I grasp at only air.

Finally discarded, I find myself amidst
the rubble and broken framework
of my reality.

I choke and open my burning eyes
to see the rest of the world
continuing on.

As I set again upon the task of living
I wonder if the next storm might
finally be my last.

WORDS

You speak to me as if
I can hear you.

Your words fall upon
my shattered eardrums,
able only to decipher
their sharpness.

The ancient brutalization
of my humanity

Has betrayed my desire
for connection, replacing
it with the need for
debilitating pain.

Your spitting and bruising
affections draw me

To you over and over again
because when you speak,
I am raw. Alive.
I am full of sensation.

I bathe in the words
that you unsheathe, showering
in their stinging nettles
as if they can somehow

Purify and restore
my soul.

ONCE

You ask me if
I ever really loved you.

I did. Early that
spring when the flowers
first broke through the earth.

I loved you when
you put your great
comforting arms around
my weary shoulders and
told me you would hold me
until the end of time.

I did. In late autumn
as the leaves turned brittle
and the air became sharp.

I loved you even as
you tore my heart from
within my breast and
discarded it for the
hope of greener evenings.

Now, as the winter whitens
the once blossoming earth
and bulbs freeze solid,

You ask me
if I loved you once.
I loved you.
I loved you once.

SENSATIONS

When she cries it is for
herself.
She cannot cry for those
she hurts.

Sometimes she studies
faces.
She mimics expressions
of humanness

And wonders what her
body is supposed to feel,
why a laugh turns up the
corners of the mouth or
tears wet the cheeks.

She weaves stories that
sound real in her mind,
stories she has pieced
together from television
and movies and books.

She makes the stories
her own.
She tells them with tears
and laughter.

She lives the life she
chooses,
the life she daily
creates.

BROKEN RHYTHMS

Loss, anger, fear, rage,
happiness,
She longs for feelings to
manifest.

Sometimes she wonders
If she is "bad" or "good"
Or if either matters at all.
They both feel the same.
Sensations reveal nothing.

BROKEN RHYTHMS

3 ENDINGS

I once pretended all stories
ended with a kiss.
Fairytales designed with
Perfect endings.

But endings are not just
beautiful things.
Sometimes, people die
alone and aching.

Crisped in the fires of
rage and age, they
are brittle and crumble
to dust, to nothingness.

I resolved to write a new
ending for my story.
Scarred, but not brittle,
nor weeping with regret.

Tattooed instead with the
memories I chose to make
and the ink I mixed with
tears and laughter and time.

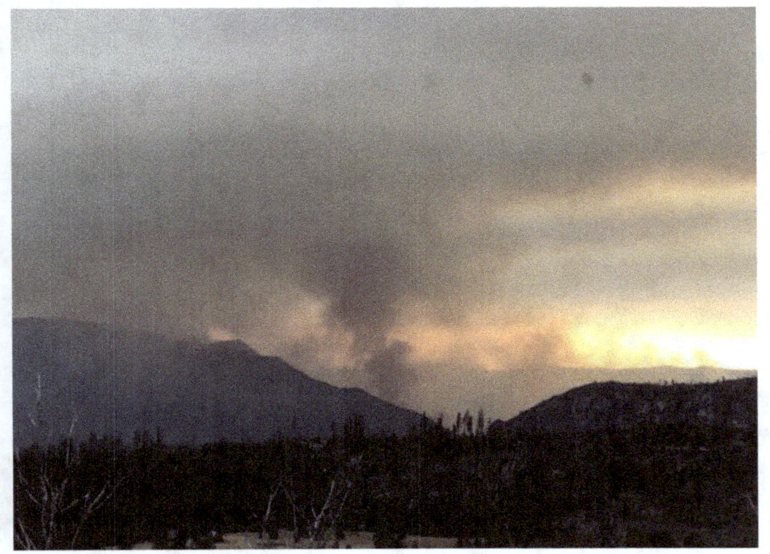

Yosemite Fires 2018

BLUE

Blue. Your eyes,
as rich as the ocean,
call me into the deep.

Filling my lungs with
salty air, I dive recklessly
into the unknown.

Curious, I explore
the dangers of
the waters.

Beautiful and new,
I am drawn far from
the surface's safety.

Vast, tumultuous and cold
they push and pull me in.
I am without direction.

Crushed by the sharp cold,
I am drowning.
There is no escape.

And so here, in foreign
and distant waters
I die.

A LITTLE DEATH

I died last night.

Well, just a small
small part of me did.

I don't know how,
but I'm less of
who or what I was.

I wonder wonder
what it was
that made me die.

It is dark
when I awaken.
I am cold and crushed.

I am in a cave
I can barely
squeeze inside.

The paintings on
the wall have been
rubbed out.

Bruised black,
they stored memories
I can no longer access.

Without them
there is no path to
the future.

Darkness.

DARK NIGHT

When you look into your soul
what do you see lurking there?
The sins of the ages exist within it,
soiled with tarry stains and maggots.

I see all of the wounds that
I could not, would not forgive.
I hear all of the whispers
of my molten anger, grinding.

Voices of yesterday curse.
Tomorrow's waiting doom hisses,
spitting through the mouths of strangers
and friends alike. Burning. Poisoning.

I watch as deceit's soft fingers
pinch the supple flesh of hope,
bruising, scarring it unrecognizable.
Death whispers rot into its ears.

From dirt to mud, we
leave only our worm-filled corpses
to be rotted into the flesh
of those who failed before.

Hope, consumed. Faith, betrayed,
the soul wastes in misguided
ventures where it is soon obliterated
by those who pretend salvation.

For until the soul makes peace
it has nothing, nor shall it
survive in the darkness,
despair pricking its delicate skin.

BROKEN RHYTHMS

I slip into the Void because
Light is best seen
through its infinite arms
and silent, eternal kiss.

CROSSING THE PILLARS

I am no longer afraid.
Death has welcomed me
with the promises of
peace, of a new journey.

The bruises of this world
are slowly fading from
my scarred skin and
blood-scathed mind.

As the shadows of this
life loom over my body,
I do not look now
behind me, for it is time

That I cross through the
great pillars to the
underworld where the
Goddess of Death awaits.

I shall certainly be harshly
judged. But no trials can
be as dark as those that
have led me to this place.

And so I cross, the
fires of Spirit singeing
my shredded soul and
embracing me home.

ETERNAL

Death sometimes sweeps into life,
surprising us with memories
we long abandoned to the past,
weaving threads of regret and
gratitude.

Life, still ours to claim in the
brilliance of the sun or the mysterious
darkness of our long shadows.
Fear, jealousy, anger, gone.
Disappeared.

It is time to remember
the goodness, the connection that
now tears our hearts within weeping
breasts and floods us with sadness.
Memories.

We are both Divine and flawed,
reaching for the Light and blind.
Touching it only through the grace
of those we love, and loved.
Eternal.

Forever is the time we spend
with Spirit. Connected to our
perfect selves and free of earthly
suffering that ends in death.
Releasing.

The veil parts and we move to
the next stage of awakening. Rebirth.
We discover truth in that place.
We discover peace, wisdom,
Agapé.

Father, Mother…
Welcome us home.

STRONGER

Trauma did not make me
stronger.
It stole my sanity, security, my
relationships, and nearly, my soul.

Trauma did not make me
wiser.
It created doubt, fear, regret
hatred and immobility.

I made a choice to grow
strong.
I fought the darkness and
blasted the shadows with light.

It was I who chose to rise
today.
To face myself and the world
around me with awakened eyes.

It was I who chose the path of the
conqueror.
To do more than survive the
assaults I couldn't see coming.

Trauma will never be my
master.
My desire to live, to thrive, to be
empowered, strengthens my soul.

VICTORIOUS

Sticks and stones
can break the bones
but words...
Words form the
wounds of the soul.

I am stronger now,
evolved from my
damaged and hated
self of year's past.

I have discovered joy,
love, beauty, and peace.

And yet in my
weakest moments,
for I still have them
now and then, the
shadows creep in.

The demons of abuse
whisper their taunts,
their disempowering
words that tug at the
stitches within
the depths of my soul.

Delicate and deceptive
memories of words I
once believed. Words
I allowed. Embodied.

Words I exposed.
Rejected.

But not without many
fierce battles, will against
words. New words against
old. Until I drew final blood.

And not without festering
flesh or seared and poisoned
bits of my very essence
exposed, raw, wasted.

Even now, the ancient
enemies' whispers tug from
deep within, picking,
searching for an opening.

Ah, but I am awake.
My warrior self stands
guard at the gates,
sword in hand and fire
in spirit to repel the
darkness as it murmurs
with masked voices.

I shall remain victorious
with new words.
Words I have chosen
to define my power.

BLOOD

Blood.
It is a poem of life, a force of nature.

As a child, I was fascinated by
the blueness of my veins,
the damaged flesh of a skinned knee,
the red, salty drops, bubbling from a torn nail.

As a woman, I feel it flowing with the cycles of the moon,
aching with every heartbeat and moving deep within me.
My clothing has been stained with its crimson beauty,
my skin smeared with the mystic power of womanhood.

And yet.
I witness this female cycle condemned,
this gift of creation made dirty and ugly.
I see girls and women ashamed,
hiding in the darkness as their life-giving blood
darkens to black in the shadows.

We, who once bled freely into the ground,
nurturing and baptizing the earth
with our bloody tithes,
to assure the fertility of the land.

We, who spread our legs to welcome the seeds of life,
sighing and calling out to the spirits seeking birth;
We, who open our yonis with the guttural sounds of creation
still enter the sacred temple and push forth life,
loud and strong,
keening in the Red.

We are Life-Blood.

BROKEN RHYTHMS

The Goddess bleeds.
If she chooses to create life
she must destroy that which she was.
In Blood.

The Goddess bleeds.
If she chooses not to create life
she must destroy that which she was.
In Blood.

And each time she bleeds,
if she welcomes the
deep red and crimson tendrils
that hold within them the very
spark of life itself,
She is Reborn.

When the blood years end,
she goes on.
She whispers her secrets
to her daughters,
and her granddaughters.

She speaks of the
great gift to her sons.
That they may revere
the Goddess and her
Sacred Blood.

She is the End.
She is the Beginning.

Conceived in a red-washed temple
and eternally adorned in blood.

4 PHOTO MEDITATIONS

Nature has always fascinated me. As a small child, I loved nothing more than listening to the rain striking the tin roof of our rental cabin in Michigan every summer at Lake Louise, or feeling the house shake when thunder rolled through.

Sunsets and sunrises were always a special time for me and remain precious moments even now. The colors and smells during that time of day bring me a peace that I find replicated only in my meditations.

Exploring photography as I have in the images here has been a way for me to capture moments that bring me pleasure and peace throughout the years, helping me rebalance and remember the beautiful moments in time that make me glad to be alive, now.

I hope you enjoy a few of them as I have.

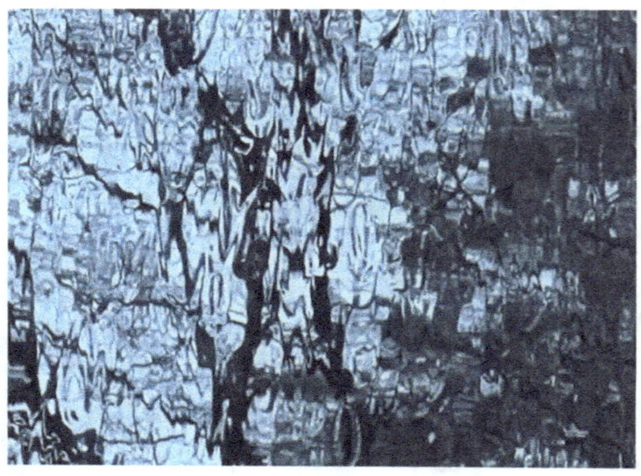

Erasing the outside world
and fingerprints from my
windowpane.
It rains.

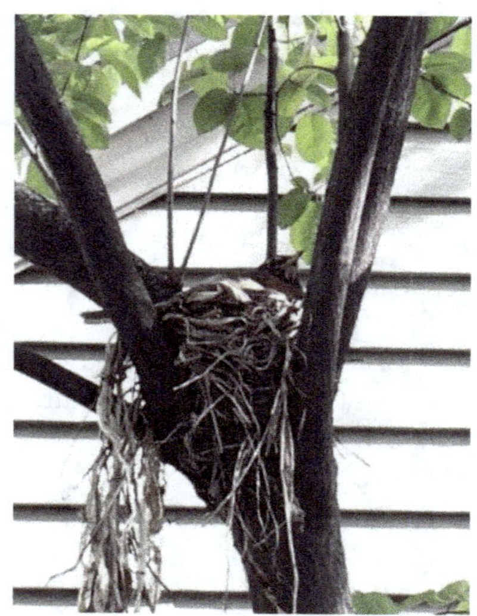

Annual guest.
A new family outside
My front door.

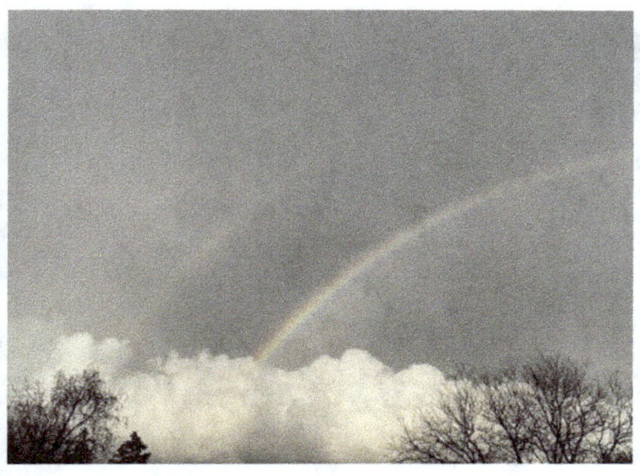

Double rainbow.
Two pots of gold for
me to find.

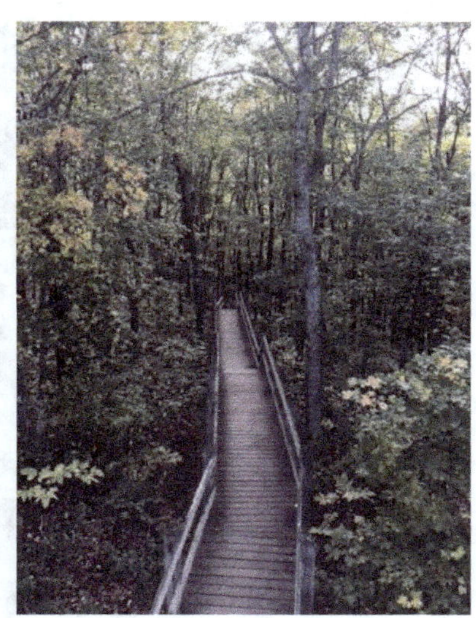

Will you trust another man's
path? Or risk venturing
into the poison ivy?

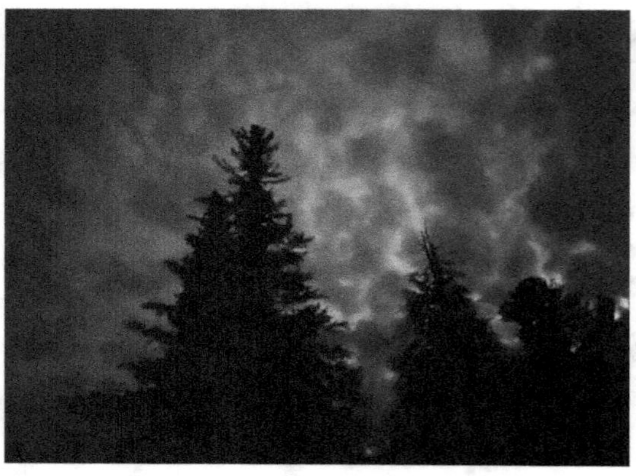

Moonlight's magickal embrace.
The clouds bear witness.

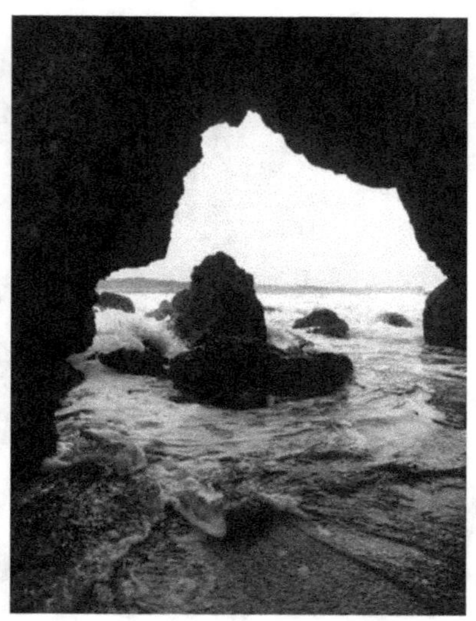

Ocean doorway.
Ancient waters
carved stone.

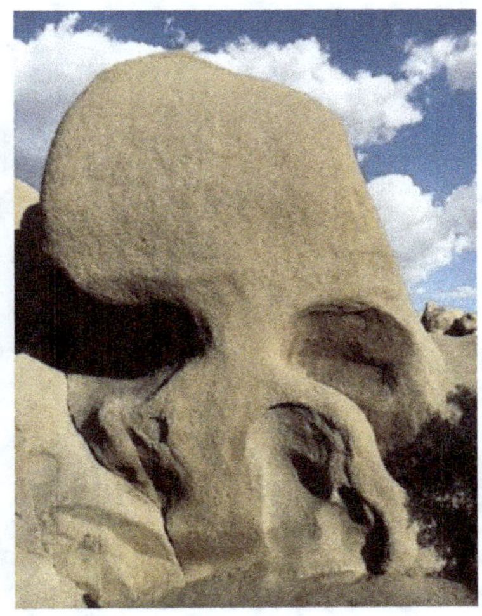

Eyes of stone
shelter stories of centuries.

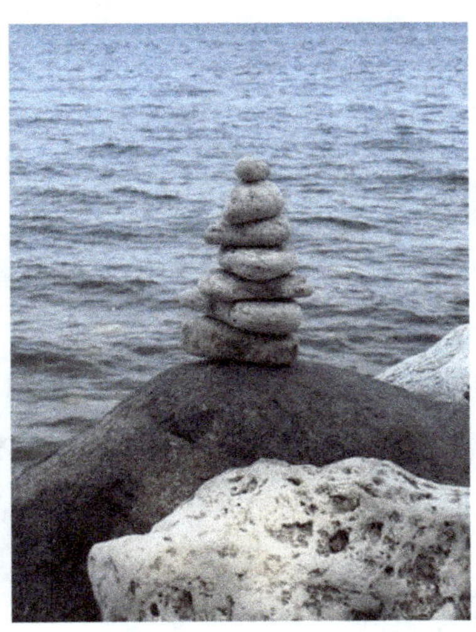

Stone, water, and wind.
Balance, harmony, and grace.

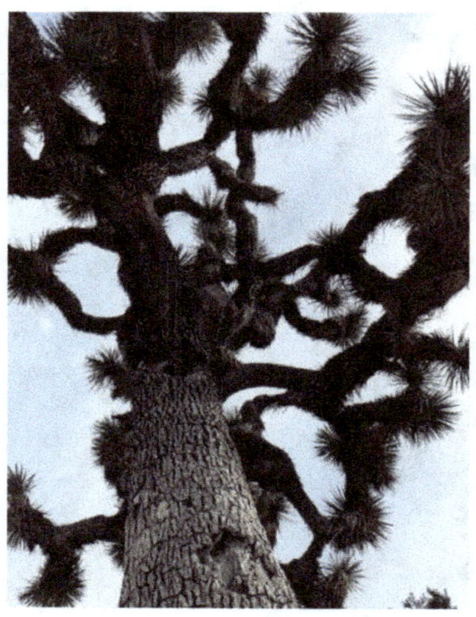

Under your outstretched arms
I rest for a few peaceful moments
in time.

Pathways to the future
too often obscured by
the past's hazy whispers.

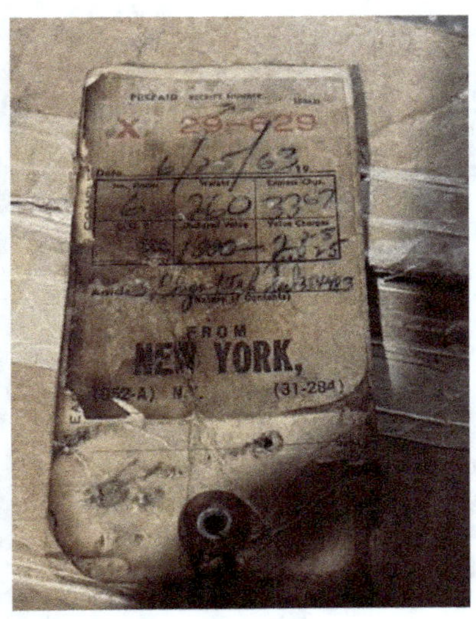

A young girl's life
about to begin
What lies in store…?

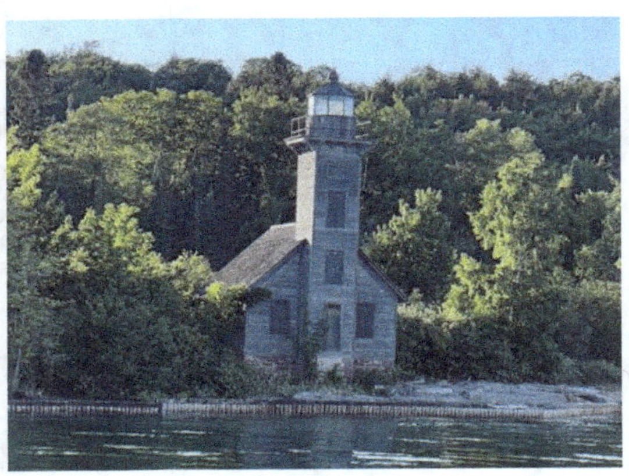

Shuttered windows
how many lives have
perished in your presence?

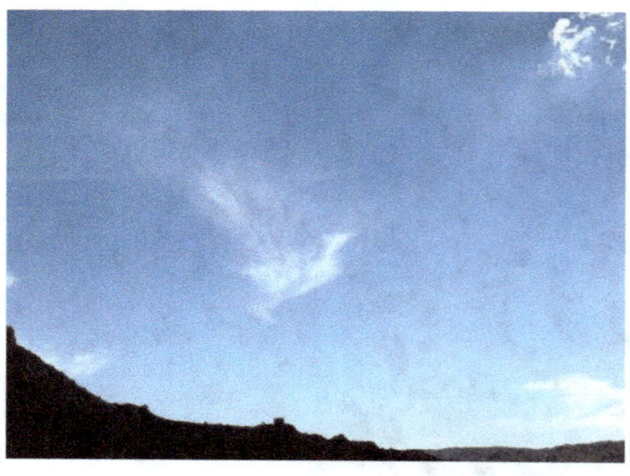

Phoenix rising.
Messengers of new life
shine from the heavens.

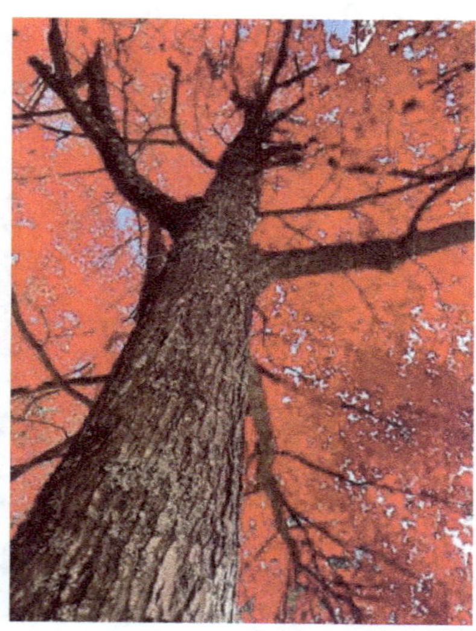

Fiery canopy.
I am enveloped
in autumn's beauty.

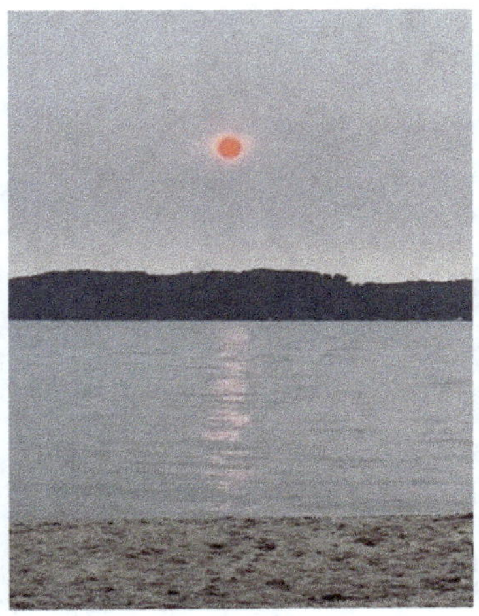

I am transported
to another world.
Pink suns and silence.

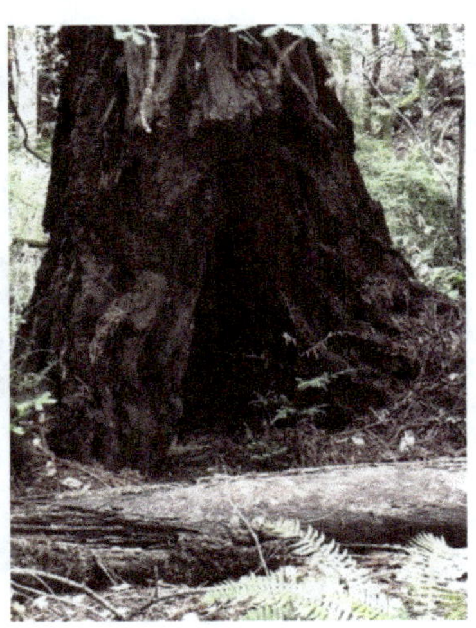

What great secrets does
this ancient dryad keep?
Spirit of the forest.

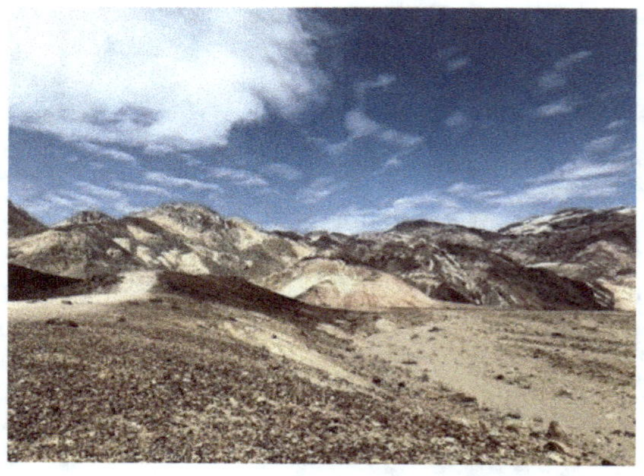

Centuries of life teeming
above and beneath
the surface.

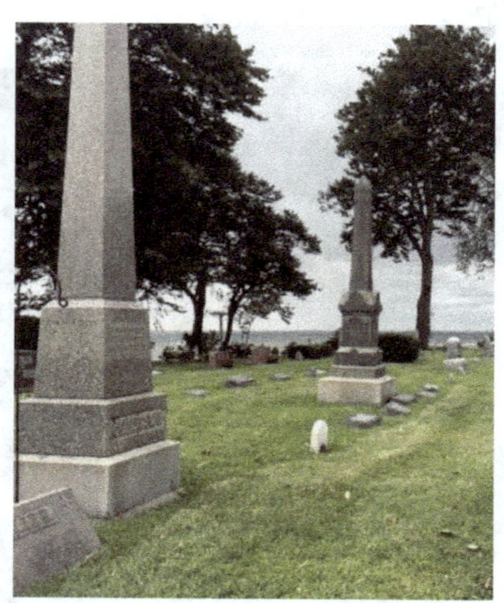

Monuments to life and death,
long forgotten,
stand and fall with time's
careless caress.

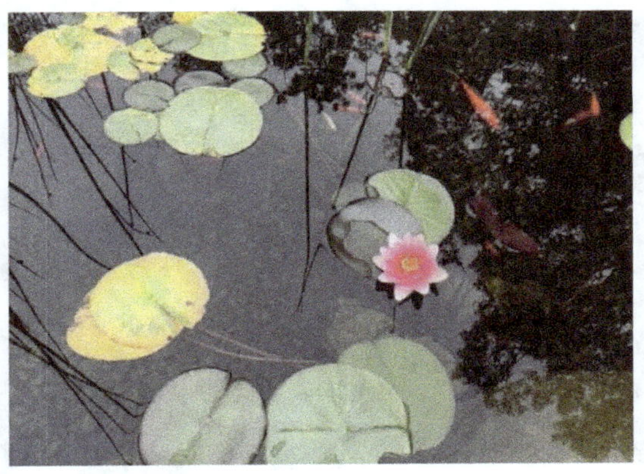

Vibrant blossom.
Nourishing to soul, spirit
and fish.

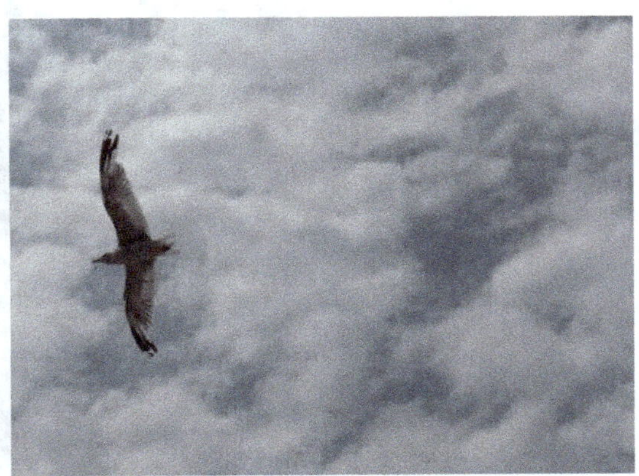

Oh, to cast aside the
density of earth
for just a moment.
If only then,
to melt my wings…

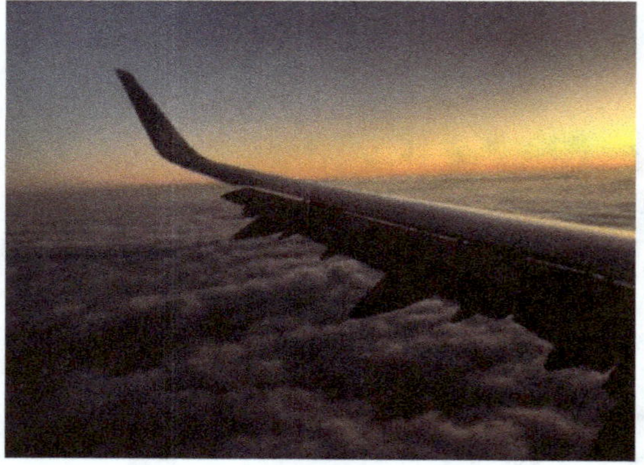

Above the earth
with the sun,
I cannot touch the clouds.

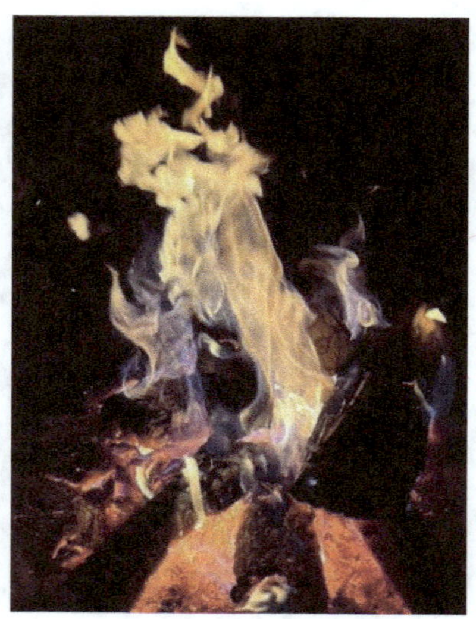

Warmth, visions, protection,
destruction, rebirth.
The mysteries of the flame.

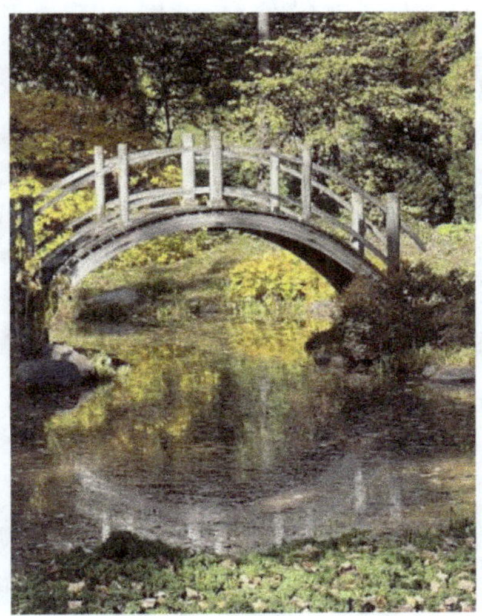

Mirrored moment.
Gateway in time to
another world.

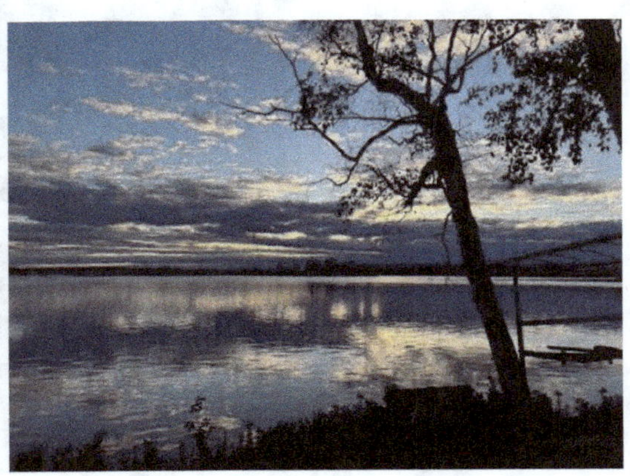

The clouds and shadows
Share a last kiss
upon the water.

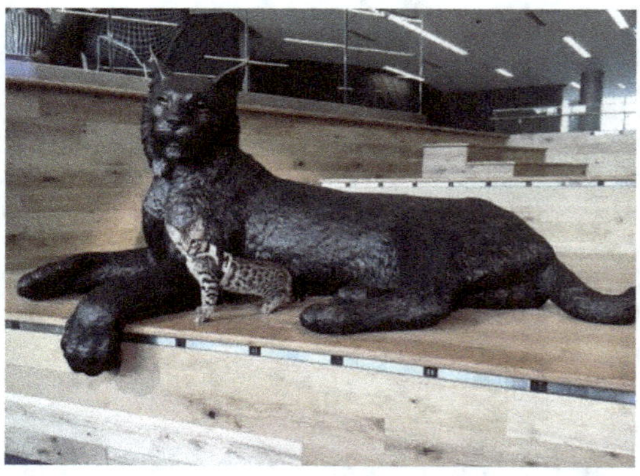

Wild and beautiful.
One just beginning
his adventure.

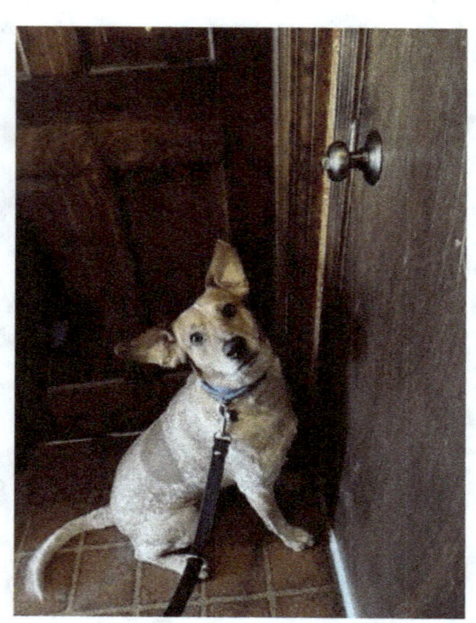

Battle scarred and alert ears
hear only the promise
of adventure.

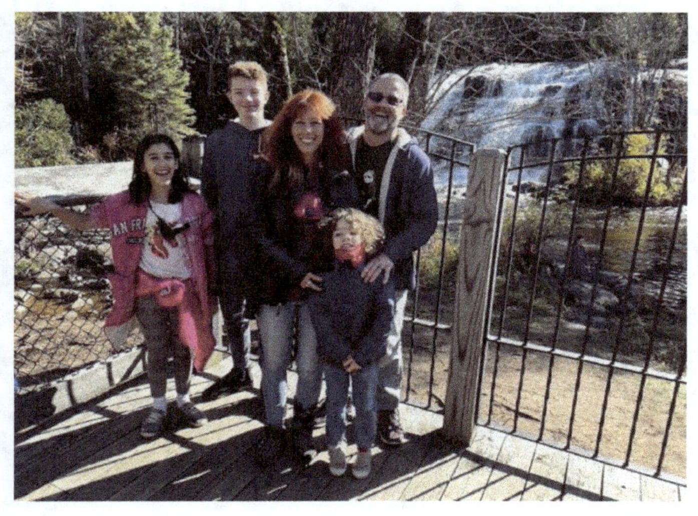

Precious gift
caught upon the lips.
A smile.

(Photo depicts the author and her family.)

5 HELPFUL TOOLS

Wherever you are on your journey, here are a few helpful tools you can use to support your path to conquering trauma.

Meditation
Meditation is a tool that has been used for centuries in to focus the mind and balance energy systems. While there are various types of meditations to explore, keeping it simple is the best way to start the process. Visualizations of a peaceful place, color or sound will immediately change the chemical processes occurring in the brain, eventually establishing a consistently quieter and stabler mind.

Focused Breathing
Studies show that there is a strong relationship between better breathing, fullness of life and longevity. Healthy breathing is also a powerful stress reliever. Once again, keeping it simple is the best way to achieve success. Three slow, deep breaths in (expanding and filing the chest, back and belly) each time followed by three slow full exhales (emptying the lungs completely) each time will quiet the

mind. Although simple, it does take practice to smoothly exercise this type of breathing. It may be done at any time.

Mindfulness

The concept of mindfulness is compiled of many tools including awareness of one's body, mind, spirit, environment, other individuals, gratitude, possibilities, and many other factors. Connection regularly to even one of these things helps keep us not only present, but also looking forward and "in motion." And movement is the only way we can effect change. Simple exercises like daily walks, conscious eating, chi do, yoga and meditation all increase awareness and active living.

TODAY

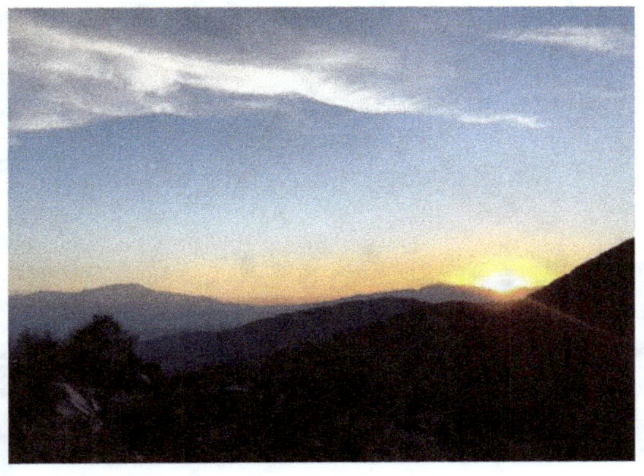

I gazed at the sky today.
I think it noticed.
It brightened and warmed the air.

I sat by the water.
I think it noticed.
It reflected my face as I leaned close.

I danced in the breeze.
I think it noticed.
It lifted me to my toes as I twirled.

I sang to the trees.
I think they noticed.
They rustled, sharing my song.

I nestled into the tall grasses.
I think they noticed.
They nurtured me with their embrace.

BROKEN RHYTHMS

I awakened to the rising moon.
I think it noticed.
It grew larger and softened the sky.

My companion barked at the setting sun.
I think it noticed.
It tumbled quickly down the mountain.

FUZZY BELLIES

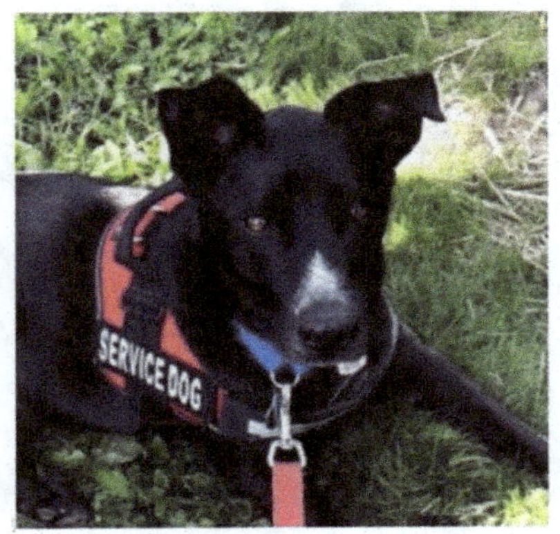

Living in service,
wide eyes that know
the truth about me,
gaze into mine.

Soft fur or feathers
and hearts bigger
than the pain I bear,
lend grace and hope.

I am accepted
as I am.

My open wounds
and wet cheeks
are nurtured, caressed
by selfless devotion.

I am free to rest,
to breathe, to quiet
my racing mind
through a soft touch.

I am grounded
and present.

Right now I can
offer you only shelter
and sustenance.
Tomorrow, more...

With your help
I am becoming
whole again.
My heart is safe.

BROKEN RHYTHMS

ABOUT THE AUTHOR

Elizabeth Selden is a post-trauma empowerment specialist, spiritual coach, educator, wife, mother, and aspiring photographer.

Diagnosed with PTSD as a young woman, she has spent her adult life exploring the most effective and long-lasting targeted techniques to reverse its effects. The careful pairing of holistic modalities such as meditation, sound therapy and etheric therapies with her interactive coaching techniques naturally regulates the brain and the body, for many, eliminating the impacts of this disorder.

This collection of poetry and photographs comes from many years of her connecting with and journaling personal traumatic experiences, as well as the beautiful ones. She shares the resonating pain experienced during many years of her life, triumphing over it in the end.

Author of Are Goddesses Real? Letters to my Daughter, creator of the **The Mind of the Conqueror** program and Creating Your Reality podcast, Elizabeth is dedicated to supporting a healing and empowering life-plan for those suffering from trauma.

She would like to dedicate these words and photographs to all those who have shined their lights through the darkness, guiding her on the path to freedom.

www.ingramcontent.com/pod-product-compliance
Lightning Source LLC
Chambersburg PA
CBHW061018260726
48661CB00005B/2232

* 9 7 9 8 8 6 2 7 1 2 5 1 3 *